Cultivating Workbook

Slant Cursive

English Lessons Through Literature

Introduction

This workbook contains all of the exercises and copywork from *English Lessons Through Literature* Level C, and space has been left for dictations and narrations as well. The instructions and occasional hints for the exercises can be found in the textbook; they are not included in the workbook.

Depending on how large your student's handwriting is, you may find that the workbook does not have enough room to complete the copywork exercise. Rather than add an additional page for the copywork passages, I elected to have one page become a natural stopping point for the copywork. Many students at this age are still developing the handwriting muscles, so this will help to keep from overworking them. For students who simply hate handwriting, you might also want to have them do only part of the handwriting pages. You could also split the copywork into up, doing a small portion each day or during several short sessions on the same day. The important thing is to give students short, regular handwriting practice as opposed to finishing reams of copywork each year. If you do have a student who wants to finish everything, a blank copywork page which you can copy is included at the back of this workbook.

The dictation pages include the dictation passage at the top of the page so that students have a copy of the passage which they can mark as they study it. This can be covered while the student is writing the passage from dictation. However, at this age, you might also leave it uncovered so that the student has a reference if help is needed. This could act as a bridge between copywork and dictation. Alternatively, the page can be for marking only if you have your student type the passage rather than write it—which is my preferred method of handling dictation.

1

He had a cow with a calf too, and an old lame horse—twenty-five years of age—and chickens, and pigeons, and two lambs, and many other animals. But his favorite pets were Dab-Dab the duck, Jip the dog, Gub-Gub the baby pig, Polynesia the parrot, and the owl Too-Too.

In the black furrow of a field
I saw an old witch-hare this night;
And she cocked her lissome ear,
And she eyed the moon so bright,

Poetry

2

quarrel

longing

bound

pay

great

Then John Dolittle got a fine,

big pair of green spectacles;

and the plow horse stopped

going blind in one eye and

could see as well as ever.

Then John Dolittle got a fine, big pair of green spectacles; and the plow horse stopped going blind in one eye and could see as well as ever.

A friend in need is a friend indeed.

The two together were able to bring the fish to land.

3

So then the Doctor's sister came to him and said, "John, you must send that creature away. Now the farmers and the old ladies are afraid to send their animals to you— just as we were beginning to be well off again."

So then the Doctor's sister came to him and said, "John, you must send that creature away. Now the farmers and the old ladies are afraid to send their animals to you—just as we were beginning to be well off again."

A man's home is his castle.

Maxim

4

"Doctor!" he cried, "I've just had a message from a cousin of mine in Africa. There is a terrible sickness among the monkeys out there. They are all catching it—and they are dying in hundreds."

cherry

box

joy

sketch

epoch

"Doctor!" he cried, "I've just had a message from a cousin of mine in Africa. There is a terrible sickness among the monkeys out there. They are all catching it—and they are dying in hundreds."

And she nibbled o' the green;
And I whispered 'Whsst! witch-hare,'
Away like a ghostie o'er the field
She fled, and left the moonlight there.

And away he ran with the body of the fish. The Otters stood and looked at each other. They had nothing to say, but each thought to himself that the Wolf had run off with the best of the fish.

"The rest of the animals, like the dormice and the water-voles and the bats, they will have to go back and live in the fields where they were born till we come home again."

holly

bay

berry

tooth

beauty

A picture is worth a thousand words.

6

Narration

Narration

7

The King opened his eyes

and said sleepily, "Is that you,

Ermintrude?" He thought it was

the Queen come back from the

dance. Then the parrot coughed

again—loud, like a man. And

the King sat up, wide awake,

and said, "Who's that?"

daddy

klutz

mommy

hooray

kiss

The King opened his eyes and said sleepily. "Is that you, Ermintrude?" He thought it was the Queen come back from the dance. Then the parrot coughed again—loud, like a man. And the King sat up, wide awake, and said, "Who's that?"

My heart leaps up when I behold
A rainbow in the sky;
So was it when my life began,
So is it now I am a man,

wise

afraid

wicked

hounds

trick

So the Leader went into

his den and looked at his

children—two very cunning

little cubs, lying on the floor.

And one of them seemed

quite poorly.

So the Leader went into his den and looked at his children—two very cunning little cubs, lying on the floor. And one of them seemed quite poorly.

Actions speak louder than words.

The world is so full of a number of things,

I'm sure we should all be as happy as kings.

9

They were very surprised at this, for they had thought that he was going to stay with them forever. And that night all the monkeys got together in the jungle to talk it over.

They were very surprised at this; for they had thought that he was going to stay with them forever. And that night all the monkeys got together in the jungle to talk it over.

Beauty is in the eye of the beholder.

10

"Yes," said the pushmi-pullyu,

"to the Abyssinian Gazelles

and the Asiatic Chamois—on

my mother's side. My father's

great-grandfather was the last

of the Unicorns."

"Yes," said the pushmi-pullyu—" to the Abyssinian Gazelles and the Asiatic Chamois—on my mother's side. My father's great-grandfather was the last of the Unicorns."

So be it when I shall grow old,
Or let me die!
The child is father of the man;
And I could wish my days to be
Bound each to each by natural piety.

Once upon a time, many, many wild Goats lived in a cave in the side of a hill. A Wolf lived with his mate not far from this cave. Like all Wolves they liked the taste of Goat-meat. So they caught the Goats, one after another, and ate them all but one who was wiser than all the others. Try as they might, the Wolves could not catch her.

Exercise

spray

butterfly

witch

candy

ray

Don't look a gift horse in the mouth.

12

Narration

Narration

13

"Good gracious! What's the matter with the dog? Is he SMELLING in his sleep—as well as talking?"

"Good gracious! What's the matter with the dog? Is he smelling in his sleep—as well as talking?"

I chatter, chatter, as I flow
  To join the brimming river;
For men may come and men may go,
  But I go on forever.

caught

traps

forest

plenty

careful

"People always speak of it

with a sneer."

And presently the canaries, who had heard all about Doctor Dolittle from birds of passage, came and led him to a beautiful spring of cool, clear water where the canaries used to take their bath; and they showed him lovely meadows where the bird-seed grew and all the other sights of their island.

Don't put all your eggs in one basket.

So Beauty and Brownie and their herds
set out. Beauty traveled at night and did
not go near any villages.

They left.

Jip shouted.

"Well," said the shark, " we know these pirates to be a bad lot—especially Ben Ali. If they are annoying you, we will gladly eat them up for you—and then you won't be troubled any more."

Every cloud has as silver lining.

Too-Too listened.

---|---

"He weeps."

---|---

He found the animals

gathered round a little door,

all talking at once, trying to

guess what was inside. The

Doctor turned the handle but

it wouldn't open. Then they

all started to hunt for the key.

They looked under the mat.

He found the animals gathered round a little door, all talking at once, trying to guess what was inside. The Doctor turned the handle but it wouldn't open. Then they all started to hunt for the key. They looked under the mat; they looked under all the carpets.

I wind about, and in and out,
With here a blossom sailing,
And here and there a lusty trout,
And here and there a grayling.

17

Two Deer named Beauty and Brownie lived with their father and mother and great herds of Deer in a forest. One day their father called them to him and said: "The Deer in the forest are always in danger when the corn is ripening in the fields. It will be best for you to go away for a while, and you must each take your own herd of Deer with you."

Then the Doctor said   You

must be mistaken, Too-Too

Half a loaf is better than no loaf.

18

Narration

19

The little boy was terribly disappointed and began to cry again, saying that no one seemed to be able to find his uncle for him. But all Jip said to the Doctor was, "Tell him that when the wind changes to the West, I'll find his uncle even though he be in China."

The little boy was terribly disappointed and began to cry again, saying that no one seemed to be able to find his uncle for him. But all Jip said to the Doctor was, "Tell him that when the wind changes to the West, I'll find his uncle even though he be in China."

I steal by lawns and grassy plots,
I slide by hazel covers;
I move the sweet forget-me-nots
That grow for happy lovers.

dispute

exploit

boastful

persuasion

hastened

He giggled.

He ran.

And she kissed the Doctor many times, so that he giggled and blushed like a school-girl. And she tried to kiss Jip too; but he ran away and hid inside the ship. "It's a silly business, this kissing," he said. "I don't hold by it. Let her go and kiss Gub-Gub—if she must kiss something."

Home is where the heart is.

Gentleness and kind persuasion win

where force and bluster fail.

21

Jip is a dog.

_____|_____

John is a doctor.

_____|_____

Even when the Doctor had filled the old money-box on the dresser-shelf, he still had a lot of money left; and he had to get three more money-boxes, just as big, to put the rest in. "Money," he said, "is a terrible nuisance. But it's nice not to have to worry."

Keep your eye on the ball.

At the very bottom he discovered some purple trousers, a red shirt and a pink vest which was dotted with white spots.

The youth was Tip.

Mombi was his guardian.

Tip boldly ransacked the great chest in which Mombi kept all her keepsakes and treasures, and at the very bottom he discovered some purple trousers, a red shirt and a pink vest which was dotted with white spots.

I slip, I slide, I gloom, I glance,
    Among my skimming swallows;
I make the netted sunbeams dance
Against my sandy shallows.

23

Then the Sun began to shine. At first his beams were gentle, and in the pleasant warmth after the bitter cold of the North Wind, the Traveler unfastened his cloak and let it hang loosely from his shoulders. The Sun's rays grew warmer and warmer. The man took off his cap and mopped his brow. At last he became so heated that he pulled off his cloak, and, to escape the blazing sunshine, threw himself down in the welcome shade of a tree by the roadside.

"Oh, yes, I can," returned Mombi. "I'm going to plant a flower garden, next Spring, and I'll put you in the middle of it, for an ornament. I wonder I haven't thought of that before; you've been a bother to me for years."

Old Mombi returned.

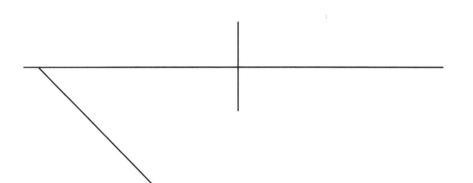

"You are a bother."

Live and let live.

24

Narration

Narration

25

"This thing resembles a real horse more than I imagined," said Tip, trying to explain. "But a real horse is alive, and trots and prances and eats oats, while this is nothing more than a dead horse, made of wood, and used to saw logs upon."

Tip reflected.

A real horse trots.

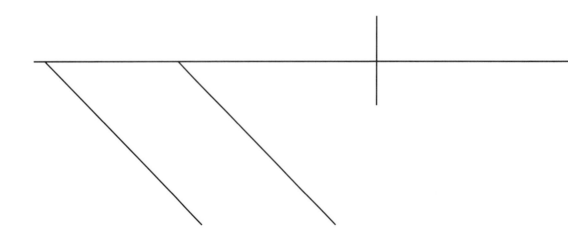

"This thing resembles a real horse more than I imagined," said Tip, trying to explain. "But a real horse is alive, and trots and prances and eats oats, while this is nothing more than a dead horse, made of wood, and used to saw logs upon."

I murmur under moon and stars
In brambly wildernesses;
I linger by my shingly bars;
I loiter round my cresses.

26

cattle

farmyard

meadow

raven

After journeying on for some distance the narrow path they were following turned into a broad roadway, paved with yellow brick. By the side of the road Tip noticed a sign post that read: "Nine Miles To The Emerald City."

They journeyed.

Tip noticed.

After journeying on for some distance the narrow path they were following turned into a broad roadway, paved with yellow brick. By the side of the road Tip noticed a sign post that read: "Nine Miles To The Emerald City."

Let sleeping dogs lie.

The lily has a smooth stalk,

Will never hurt your hand;

But the rose upon her briar

Is lady of the land.

27

Sparkling green gems ornamented the fronts of the beautiful houses and the towers and turrets were all faced with emeralds. Even the green marble pavement glittered with precious stones, and it was indeed a grand and marvelous sight to one who beheld it for the first time.

The man laughed.

That horse is wood.

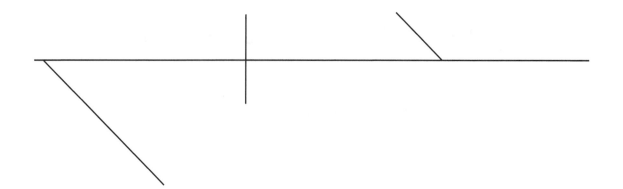

Sparkling green gems ornamented the fronts of the beautiful houses and the towers and turrets were all faced with emeralds. Even the green marble pavement glittered with precious stones, and it was indeed a grand and marvelous sight to one who beheld it for the first time.

Look before you leap.

28

"He says that your Majesty's

brains seem to have come

loose," replied the girl,

demurely.

The Scarecrow moved.

Indignant Jack protested.

"What does he say?" inquired the Scarecrow. "My ears must have deceived me. What did he say?"

"He says that your Majesty's brains seem to have come loose," replied the girl, demurely.

And out again I curve and flow
To join the brimming river;
For men may come and men may go,
But I go on forever.

29

"Don't you know?" cried the raven. "I have watched your cattle all day long, and have now brought them home safe in the evening."

"Do you mean to say you have done all this work for me?" asked the farmer.

"To be sure I have," said the raven. Then off he flew.

"Well," said the farmer, as he watched the bird fly out of sight, "how many there are that take credit for things that they have never done!"

"I am General Jinjur."

Tip laughed.

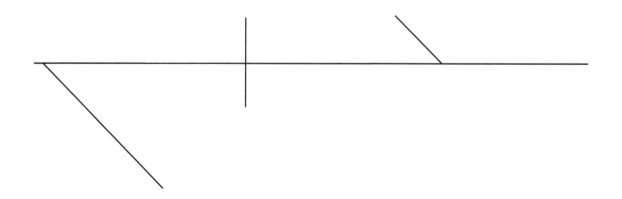

"The army is feeble."

Necessity is the mother of invention.

30

Narration

Narration

31

The horse obeyed.

The Scarecrow groaned.

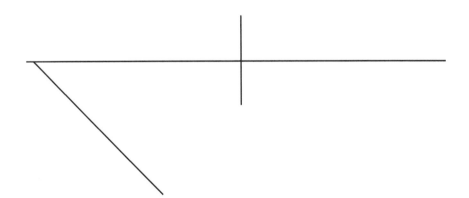

"There are several distinct advantages in being a Scarecrow. For if one has friends near at hand to repair damages, nothing very serious can happen to you."

Slowly, silently, now the moon
Walks the night in her silver shoon:
This way, and that, she peers and sees
Silver fruit upon silver trees;

32

cobbler

basement

mend

trust

gold

"How delighted I shall be

to see my old friend the Tin

Woodman again!"

"He is a proud man."

"You are unusual."

The Scarecrow became greatly animated at this sight, and exclaimed: "How delighted I shall be to see my old friend the Tin Woodman again! I hope that he rules his people more successfully than I have ruled mine!"

Nothing ventured, nothing gained.

The next day, dressed in the skin, the Wolf strolled into the pasture with the Sheep.

33

Tip had played a trick on Mombi.

Mombi was furious.

"My anatomy is brittle."

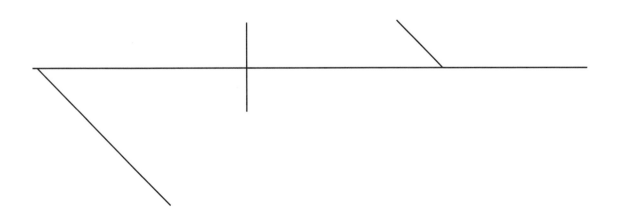

Mombi was furious at the trick Tip had played upon her as well as at his escape and the theft of the precious Powder of Life; so she needed no urging to induce her to travel to the Emerald City to assist Jinjur in defeating the Scarecrow and the Tin Woodman, who had made Tip one of their friends.

A chain is only as strong as its weakest link.

34

Did the young scholars yell?

Did the students stand?

"My action, being unexpected, must have startled them, for one of the little girls perched upon the window-sill gave a scream and fell backward out the window, drawing her companion with her as she disappeared."

One by one the casements catch
Her beams beneath the silvery thatch;
Couched in his kennel, like a log,
With paws of silver sleeps the dog
From their shadowy cote the white breasts peep

35

"Dear husband," she said, "take back the gold. All the gold in the world is not worth as much to me as one of your old glad songs."

How happy the cobbler felt just to hear her say this! He picked up the purse and ran upstairs to the rich man's room. Throwing the gold on the table, he cried: "Here is your money. Take it back. I can live without your money, but I cannot live without my song."

Were the scholars students?

Is Nick the Tin Woodman?

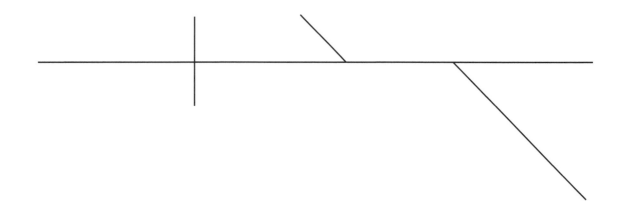

Out of sight, out of mind.

36

Narration

37

"This terrible Queen Jinjur

suggested making a goulash of me."

Is Jinjur Queen?

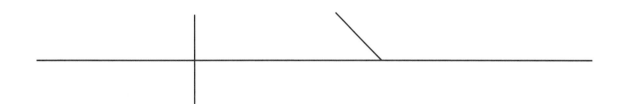

The Woggle-Bug groaned.

"But I hope she cannot get at us,"
exclaimed the Pumpkinhead, with a
shiver of fear. "She threatened to make
tarts of me, you know."

"Don't worry," said the Tin Woodman.
"It cannot matter greatly. If you stay shut
up here you will spoil in time, anyway.
A good tart is far more admirable than a
decayed intellect."

Of doves in a silver-feathered sleep;
A harvest mouse goes scampering by,
With silver claws and silver eye;
And moveless fish in the water gleam
By silver reeds in a silver stream.

thrush

wiry

grub

bough

bark

The monarch and his friends listened.

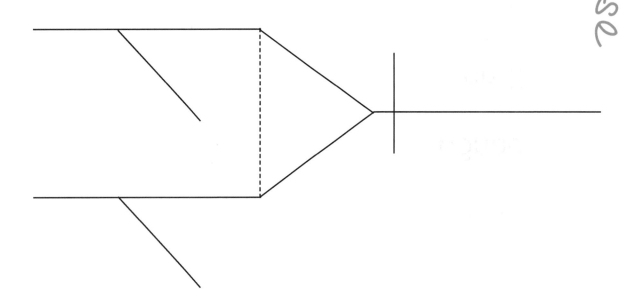

He and his burden tumbled.

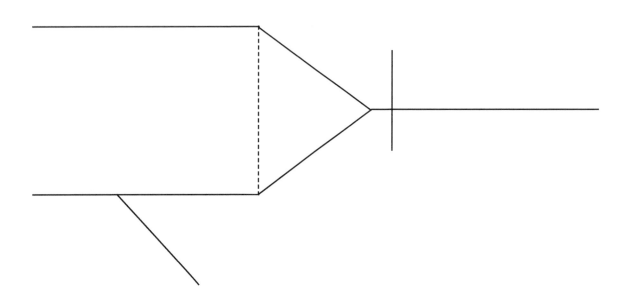

It was now that the wisdom of the Scarecrow, in bringing the head of the Thing to life instead of the legs, was proved beyond a doubt. For the Gump, already high in the air, turned its head at Tip's command and gradually circled around until it could view the roof of the palace.

Patience is a virtue.

"He is eating ants," said Peggy. "The tip of his tongue is sticky and he draws them into his mouth."

39

The Gump landed and turned.

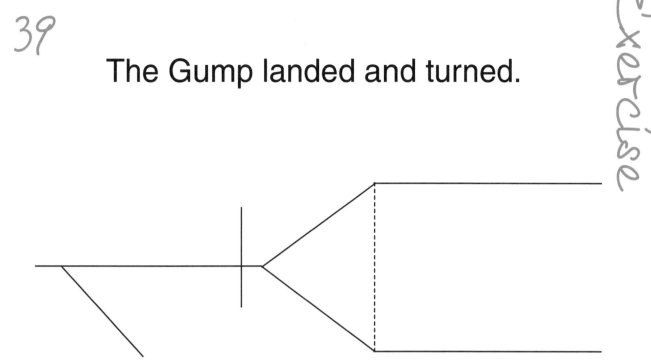

The Pumpkinhead and the

Woggle-Bug moaned and feared.

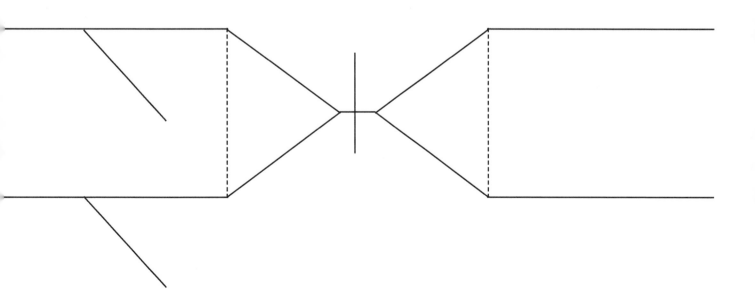

"Yet here I am, alive again, with four monstrous wings and a body which I venture to say would make any respectable animal or fowl weep with shame to own. What does it all mean? Am I a Gump, or am I a juggernaut?" The creature, as it spoke, wiggled its chin whiskers in a very comical manner.

Silence is golden.

40

The jackdaws threatened the

Tin Woodman's brilliant plating.

Can they use the wishing pills?

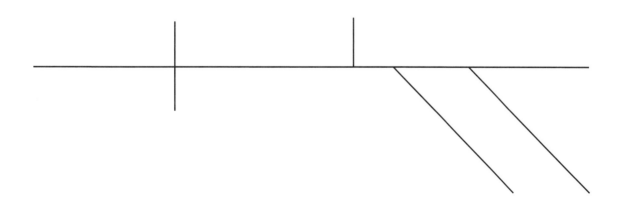

They selected all the newest and cleanest bills and assorted them into various piles. The Scarecrow's left leg and boot were stuffed with five-dollar bills; his right leg was stuffed with ten-dollar bills, and his body so closely filled with fifties, one-hundreds and one-thousands that he could scarcely button his jacket with comfort.

Wide are the meadows of night,
And daisies are shining there,
Tossing their lovely dews,
Lustrous and fair;

41

So we lay quite still under the tree. Soon the sound came nearer, and a great heavy bird, bigger than a large thrush, flew towards us. He was a beautiful bird. His wings were green, and so was his breast. He had yellow on his tail. His head was red, and he had a red streak on his throat. His beak was long and grey.

It waved its broom tail.

An educated Woggle-Bug is a

new thing.

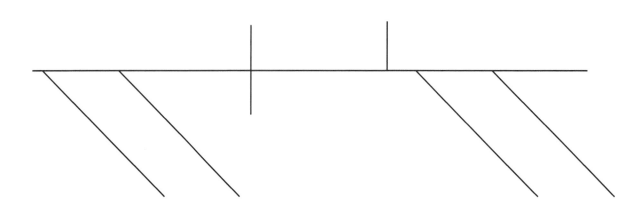

Slow and steady wins the race.

42

Narration

43

The Scarecrow searched his

pocket.

"The houses and fences are

blue."

January	Jan.	July	Jul.
February	Feb.	August	Aug.
March	Mar.	September	Sep.
April	Apr.	October	Oct.
May	May	November	Nov.
June	Jun.	December	Dec.

And through these sweet fields go,
Wanderers amid the stars—
Venus, Mercury, Uranus, Neptune,
Saturn, Jupiter, Mars.

squirrel

shy

autumn

snug

cozy

"Tell your Queen."

"Answer me!"

"Tell your mistress that I cannot find Mombi anywhere, but that Glinda is welcome to enter the city and search herself for the old woman. She may also bring her friends with her, if she likes; but if she does not find Mombi by sundown, the Sorceress must promise to go away peaceably and bother us no more."

Strike while the iron is hot.

He never stops, but slackens

Above the Ripest Rose-

Partakes without alighting

And praises as he goes.

45

She was comfortably reading

a novel.

The Sorceress turned quickly.

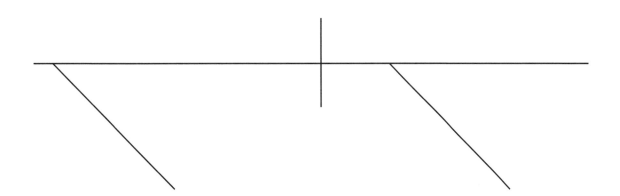

"I am," returned the Scarecrow, "but not on account of my money. For I consider brains far superior to money, in every way. You may have noticed that if one has money without brains, he cannot use it to advantage; but if one has brains without money, they will enable him to live comfortably to the end of his days."

The best things in life are free.

46

"Do you not believe?"

Macbeth's son would not rule.

The Queen dared not permit an answer to be given to this question. She hurriedly begged her guests to quit a sick man who was likely to grow worse if he was obliged to talk.

'Tired in their silver, they move,
And circling, whisper and say,
Fair are the blossoming meads of delight
Through which we stray.

His back is covered with a brown red fur,
but under his body the fur is white.
His lovely red tail is like a brush on his
back. His hind legs are long. That is why
he can jump so well. On his front paws
one toe stands out from the others, almost
like our thumb. He uses his paws like
hands, when he sits up with a nut in
them, and peels off the brown skin with
his teeth.

He hadn't seen the right lady.

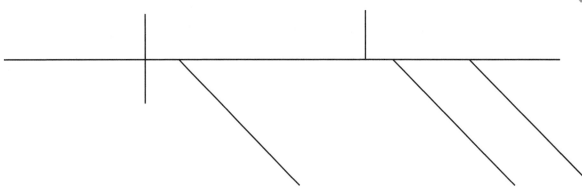

He's Romeo.

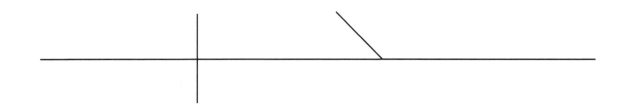

The early bird catches the worm.

48

Narration

49

He made heavenly music.

He forgave them.

Sunday	Sun.
Monday	Mon.
Tuesday	Tue. or Tues.
Wednesday	Wed.
Thursday	Thu. or Thurs.
Friday	Fri.
Saturday	Sat.

Copywork

The blossoms will be gone in the winter:
Oh apples, come for the June!
Can you come, will you bloom?
Will you stay till the cold?

orchard

bulb

autumn

anemones

poisonous

"He left this ring."

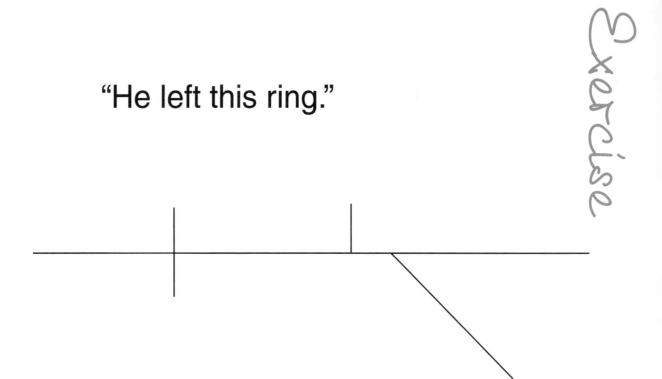

"She never told her love."

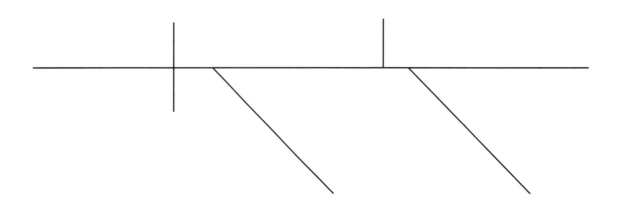

Viola, however (who was now called Cesario), refused to take any denial, and vowed to have speech with the Countess. Olivia, hearing how her instructions were defied and curious to see this daring youth, said, "We'll once more hear Orsino's embassy."

The future is now.

But we cannot get a good bunch until April. Before that the plants are busy growing their leaves.

51

Fairies attended Bottom.

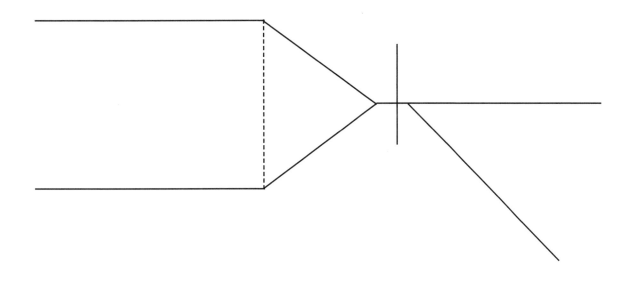

King and Queen live happily.

"Now, sit down with me," said the Queen to the clown, "and let me stroke your dear cheeks, and stick musk-roses in your smooth, sleek head, and kiss your fair large ears, my gentle joy."

There is safety in numbers.

52

Now Hamlet had offended his

uncle and his mother.

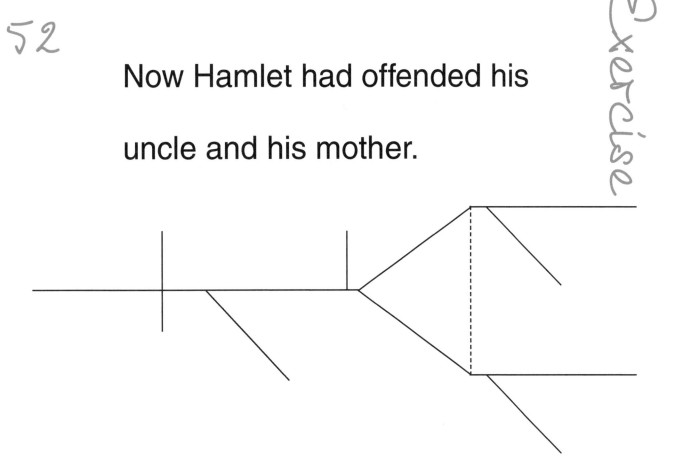

His son grieves still.

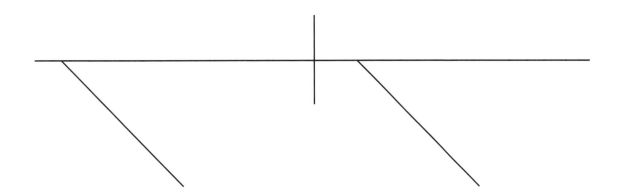

So when his friends came back he made them swear to keep the secret of the ghost, and then went in from the battlements, now gray with mingled dawn and moonlight, to think how he might best avenge his murdered father.

Boats sail on the rivers,
And ships sail on the seas;
But clouds that sail across the sky
Are prettier far than these.

53

The first bright flowers we find are the
daffodils in the fields, and the anemones
in the woods. They have very long,
narrow leaves which come straight out of
the ground. Each flower hangs on its own
tall stalk. It has deep yellow tube in the
middle, with a crown of pale yellow leaves
round it. If you dig up a daffodil plant
you will find that it has a bulb like an
onion. It stores up food in the bulb in
the autumn. Then it uses this food in
January to make its leaves and flowers.

The family lived abroad.

She hid upstairs.

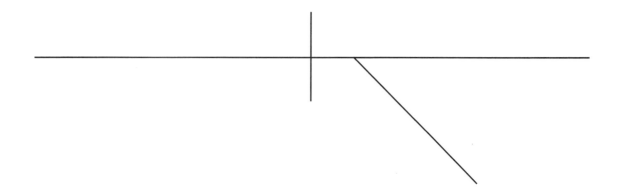

There's no place like home.

54

Narration

55

He was always teasing his

sisters.

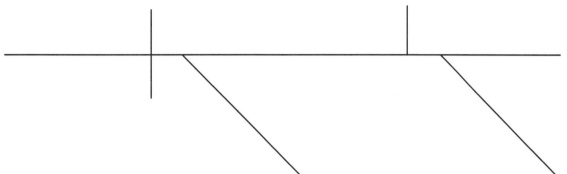

"You have had a sleep!"

The horses were climbing up a hilly piece of road when she first caught sight of a light. Mrs. Medlock saw it as soon as she did and drew a long sigh of relief.

There are bridges on the rivers,
As pretty as you please;
But the bow that bridges heaven,
And overtops the trees,
And builds a road from earth to sky,
Is prettier far than these.

perhaps

amuse

brisk

canter

acquaint

She moved softly.

Suddenly a rippling sound broke out.

"Would you make friends with me?"
she said to the robin just as if she was
speaking to a person. "Would you?" And
she did not say it either in her hard
little voice or in her imperious Indian
voice.

There's no such thing as a free lunch.

"Oh, if that is what you wish," said King Henry, "get up behind me on the horse, and I'll take you to the place where you will see him."

57

She had just paused.

It's very queer.

She had felt as if she had understood a robin and that he had understood her; she had run in the wind until her blood had grown warm; she had been healthily hungry for the first time in her life; and she had found out what it was to be sorry for some one. She was getting on.

Too many cooks spoil the broth.

Martha ran and shut the door

and turned the key.

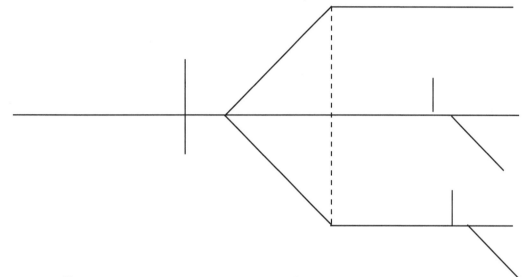

She went out and slammed

the door.

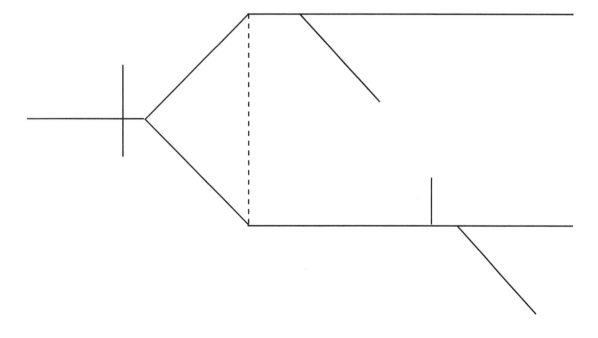

She went out of the room and slammed the door after her, and Mary went and sat on the hearth-rug, pale with rage. She did not cry, but ground her teeth.

Sea-shell, Sea-shell,
Sing me a song, oh! Please!
A song of ships, and sailormen,
And parrots, and tropical trees;
Of islands lost in the Spanish Main,

59

"No, sir," answered the boy. "I am looking for the king. They say he is hunting in the woods and perhaps will ride out this way. So I'm waiting to see him."

"Oh, if that is what you wish," said King Henry, "get up behind me on the horse and I'll take you to the place where you will see him."

Two wrongs don't make a right.

"Oh! Is it you?"

Why, it was a key!

60

Narration

61

"Oh! You're a good girl!"

"It isn't a quite dead garden."

"If I have a spade," she whispered, "I can make the earth nice and soft and dig up weeds. If I have seeds and can make flowers grow the garden won't be dead at all—it will come alive."

Which no man ever may find again,
Of fishes and corals under the waves,
And seahorses stabled in great green caves.
Oh, Sea-shell, Sea-shell,
Sing of the things you know so well.

rude

hut

haste

ragged

hearth

"Eh! It is a queer, pretty place!"

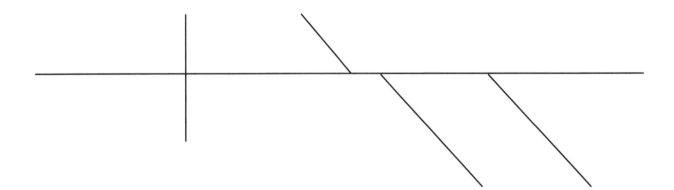

"It's a secret garden."

"I don't care, I don't care! Nobody has any right to take it from me when I care about it and they don't. They're letting it die, all shut in by itself," she ended passionately, and she threw her arms over her face and burst out crying—poor little Mistress Mary.

Waste not, want not.

She sings across the waters clear

And dark with trees and stars between,

The notes her fairy godmother

Taught her, the child Evangeline.

63

"We must talk low."

"Oh! I forgot!"

For two or three minutes he stood looking round him, while Mary watched him, and then he began to walk about softly, even more lightly than Mary had walked the first time she had found herself inside the four walls.

Don't change horses in midstream.

64

"She knows all about children."

"Oh! I'm so glad!"

He was watching her.

"A bit of earth," he said to himself, and Mary thought that somehow she must have reminded him of something. When he stopped and spoke to her his dark eyes looked almost soft and kind.

Let us walk in the white snow
In a soundless space;
With footsteps quiet and slow,
At a tranquil pace,
Under veils of white lace.

"Martha knew about you all

the time?"

"Shut your eyes."

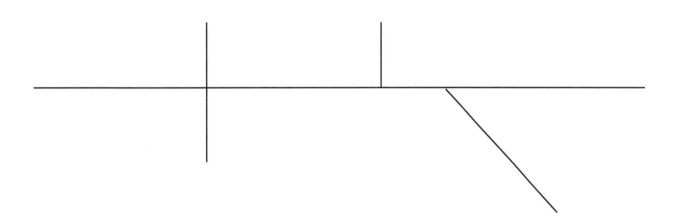

"I am Colin."

Hindsight is better than foresight.

66

Narration

Mary flew across the grass to him.

"I am a boy animal."

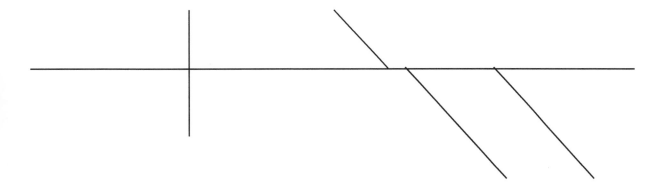

Mary looked and caught her breath.

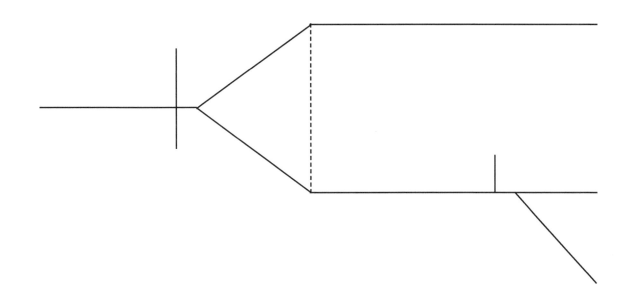

In her talks with Colin, Mary had tried to be very cautious about the secret garden. There were certain things she wanted to find out from him, but she felt that she must find them out without asking him direct questions.

I shall go shod in silk,
And you in wool,
White as a white cow's milk,
More beautiful
Than the breast of a gull.

state

ruler

brief

laconic

master

"He's a common cottage boy

off the moor!"

"I am very busy."

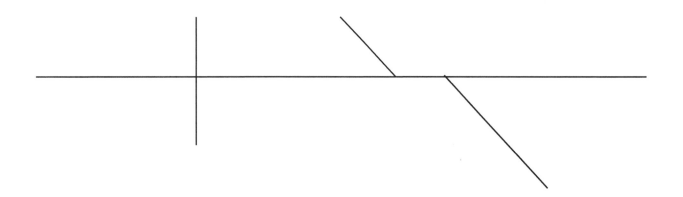

"You are a selfish thing!"

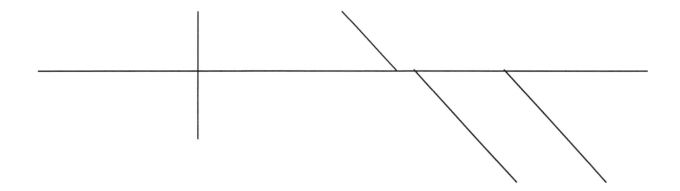

"I'm getting fatter and fatter every day," she said quite exultantly. "Mrs. Medlock will have to get me some bigger dresses. Martha says my hair is growing thicker. It isn't so flat and stringy."

The pen is mightier than the sword.

And so a short answer is often spoken of as being laconic.

69

"She knows all about children."

"I can't bear it."

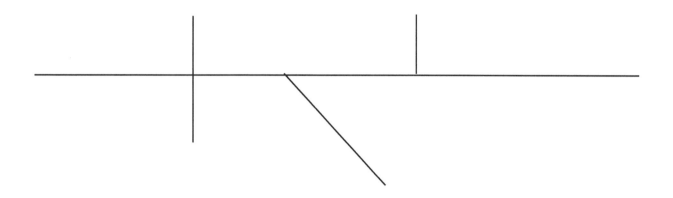

"You go and scold him."

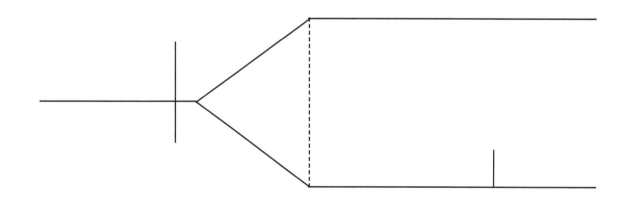

She flew along the corridor and the nearer she got to the screams the higher her temper mounted. She felt quite wicked by the time she reached the door. She slapped it open with her hand and ran across the room to the four-posted bed.

You can't have your cake and eat it too.

70

He clutched her hands and

dragged her toward him.

"Shall I see it?"

"Well, Dickon will come tomorrow."

If he had been a strong healthy boy, Colin would probably have shouted, "Hooray! Hooray! Hooray!" But he was weak and rather hysterical; his eyes grew bigger and bigger and he gasped for breath.

We shall walk through the still town
In a windless peace;
We shall step upon white down,
Upon silver fleece,
Upon softer than these.

71

Philip of Macedon wanted to become the master of all Greece. So he raised a great army, and made war upon the other states, until nearly all of them were forced to call him their king. Then he sent a letter to the Spartans in Laconia, and said, "If I go down into your country, I will level your great city to the ground."

She was fond of Susan Sowerby.

The nurse gave a slight gasp.

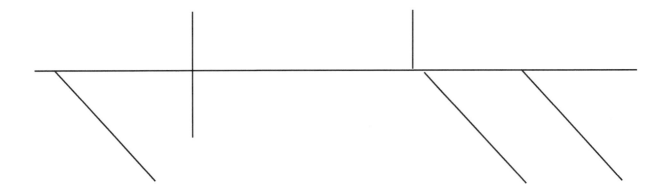

"She's a shrewd woman."

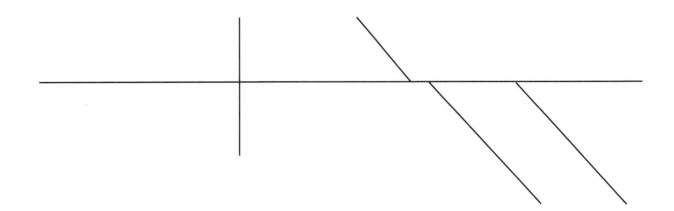

You can't judge a book by its cover.

72

Narration

73

They drew the chair under the plum-tree, which was snow-white with blossoms and musical with bees.

Delight reigned.

Delight | reigned

They were safe.

They | were | safe

"I'm going to get nothing else," he answered. "I've seen the spring now and I'm going to see the summer. I'm going to see everything grow here. I'm going to grow here myself."

We shall walk in velvet shoes:
Wherever we go
Silence will fall like dews
On white silence below.
We shall walk in the snow.

caste

afford

tirelessly

grasp

concoct

Between the blossoming branches of the canopy bits of blue sky looked down like wonderful eyes.

"Have I got crooked legs?"

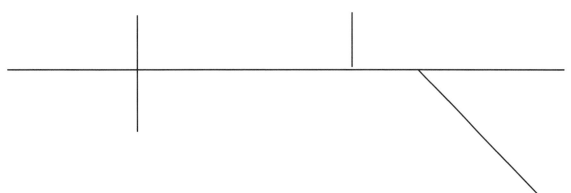

"Go and meet him."

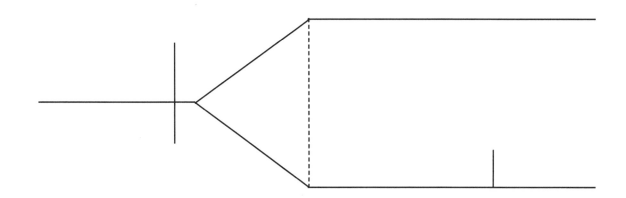

"It is my garden now, I am fond of it. I shall come here every day," announced Colin. "But it is to be a secret. My orders are that no one is to know that we come here. Dickon and my cousin have worked and made it come alive."

You can't take it with you.

She was the talk of the village because although she was but a single thin woman, she would use the money she earned to buy enough rice to feed ten people!

75

Write a list of at least three things. It can be favorite toys, books, or foods. It can be things that annoy you most. It can be most disgusting things your sibling does. It can be things your household needs from the grocery store. Just make it at least three items and use commas to separate your list items.

The Rajah waved his hand.

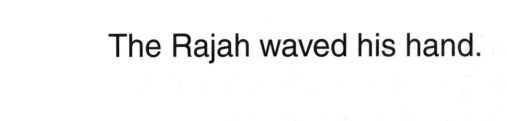

"I shall be a Scientific

Discoverer."

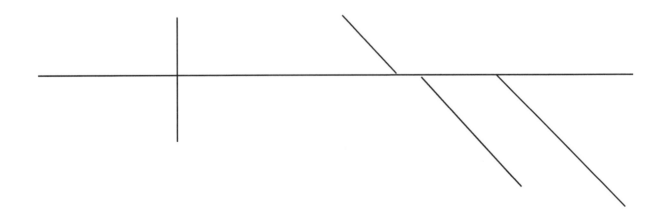

Dickon held his rabbit in his arm, and perhaps he made some charmer's signal no one heard, for when he sat down, cross-legged like the rest, the crow, the fox, the squirrels and the lamb slowly drew near and made part of the circle, settling each into a place of rest as if of their own desire.

The squeaky wheel gets the grease.

76

It was in these twilight hours

that Mrs. Sowerby heard

of all that happened at

Misselthwaite Manor.

She asked many questions.

"Dickon, you are the most

Magic boy!"

So one beautiful still evening Dickon told the whole story, with all the thrilling details of the buried key and the robin and the gray haze which had seemed like deadness and the secret Mistress Mary had planned never to reveal.

I was bare as a leaf
And I felt the wind on my shoulder.
The trees laughed
When I picked up the sun in my fingers.
The wind was chasing the waves,
Tangling their white curls.

77

The next evening, they did just that, cooking their rice and then sitting down to eat it in the dark. But instead of picking up her spoon, the younger sister darted out her hand and grabbed at the air. And instead of passing through nothing, her hand grasped around a lock of hair, and she quickly told her sister to turn on the lamp.

"I won't have letters written to my father—I won't—I won't! You are making me angry, and you know that is bad for me."

Mary giggled inordinately.

"Ring the bell."

Where there's a will there's a way.

78

Narration

79

Exercise

And so they led him in.

He was remembering the dream.

"Aren't you glad, Father?"

Much more surprising things can happen to any one who, when a disagreeable or discouraged thought comes into his mind, just has the sense to remember in time and push it out by putting in an agreeable, determinedly courageous one. Two things cannot be in one place.

"Where you tend a rose, my lad,
A thistle cannot grow."

"Willow trees," I said,
"O willows,
Look at your lake!
Stop laughing at a little girl
Who runs past your feet in the sand!"

inhabited

notorious

predicament

rupee

calamity

Now in these subterranean caverns lived a strange race of beings, called by some gnomes, by some kobolds, by some goblins.

She did not cry long.

She wiped her eyes.

One very wet day, when the mountain was covered with mist which was constantly gathering itself together into rain-drops, and pouring down on the roofs of the great old house, whence it fell in a fringe of water from the eaves all round about it, the princess could not of course go out.

Variety is the spice of life.

There was an Old Man with a beard,

Who said, "It is just as I feared!—

Two owls and a hen,

Four larks and a wren,

Have all built their nests in my beard!"

81

"But I never saw you before."

"Hadn't you a handkerchief, child?"

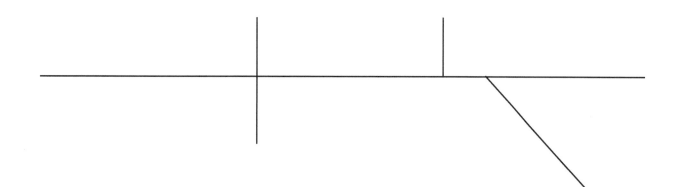

"Do you know my name?"

When she carried away the basin and towel, the little princess wondered to see how straight and tall she was, for, although she was so old, she didn't stoop a bit. She was dressed in black velvet with thick white heavy-looking lace about it; and on the black dress her hair shone like silver.

United we stand, divided we fall.

82

And indeed today is very seldom like yesterday, if people would note the differences—even when it rains.

"Oh, I daresay!"

"I'm not talking nonsense."

Her failure to find the old lady not only disappointed her, but made her very thoughtful. Sometimes she came almost to the nurse's opinion that she had dreamed all about her; but that fancy never lasted very long.

Smooth it glides upon its travel,
Here a wimple, there a gleam—
O the clean gravel!
O the smooth stream!

83

The merchants were in quite the predicament, tied up with all of their belongings stolen. The robbers, on the other hand, were quite pleased with themselves and were so full of pride for their daring crime that they began to have very inflated opinions of themselves. They fancied themselves as kings, and as the sun set, they demanded that their prisoners be untied and dance for them.

"I've been up a long way to see my very great, huge, old grandmother," said the princess.

A real princess is never rude.

She did not say it crossly.

Two heads are better than one.

84

Narration

85

He saw no more of the

goblins, and was soon fast

asleep in his bed.

"Oh! It's not much."

_____

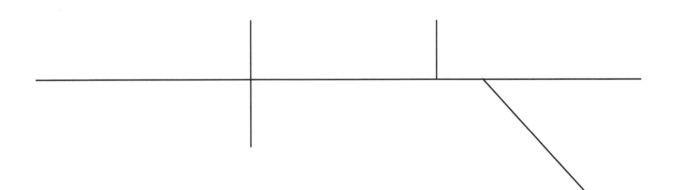

"I'll do my best."

First, he wanted to get extra wages in order that he might buy a very warm red petticoat for his mother, who had begun to complain of the cold of the mountain air sooner than usual this autumn; and second, he had just a faint glimmering of hope of finding out what the goblins were about under his window the night before.

Sailing blossoms, silver fishes,
Pave pools as clear as air—
How a child wishes
To live down there!

exquisite

despair

painstaking

pyre

cremate

"He's by no means at the

thinnest place."

A deeper voice replied.

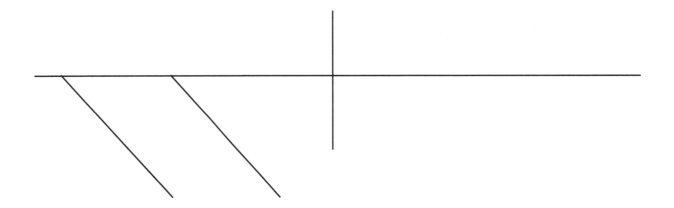

"It's awfully heavy."

"What a distinction it is to provide our own light, instead of being dependent on a thing hung up in the air—a most disagreeable contrivance—intended no doubt to blind us when we venture out under its baleful influence!"

When in Rome, do as the Romans do.

"That is a very dangerous place for you," he called out, pretending to be very anxious about the Goat's safety. "What if you should fall! Please listen to me and come down! Here you can get all you want of the finest, tenderest grass in the country."

87

Well might he wish that he

had brought his lamp and

tinder-box with him.

He started back.

He hurried on.

The floor was rough and stony; the walls full of projecting corners; the roof in one place twenty feet high, in another endangering his forehead; while on one side a stream, no thicker than a needle, it is true, but still sufficient to spread a wide dampness over the wall, flowed down the face of the rock.

You win some and you lose some.

88

She jumped up with a cry of joy.

"We'll have a walk."

The garden was a very lovely place.

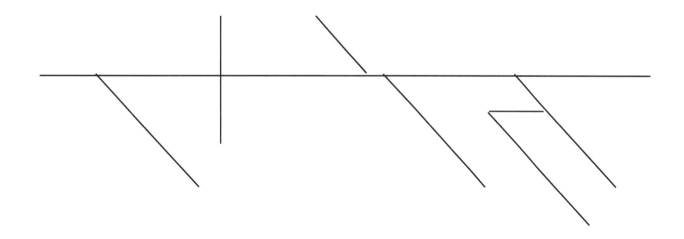

It was a long time since he had been to see her, and her little heart beat faster and faster as the shining troop approached, for she loved her king-papa very dearly, and was nowhere so happy as in his arms.

We can see our colored faces
Floating on the shaken pool
Down in cool places,
Dim and very cool;

89

The wife agreed, and so they both lay down, keeping their ears open to hear any cheating from the other. First the minutes ticked by. Then, the hours. And as they both lay there stubbornly refusing to forfeit that last muffin, days slipped by.

The moon was shining brightly into the room. The poultice had fallen off her hand, and it was burning hot.

Her nurse Lootie left her.

( )

The princess loved her father the king.

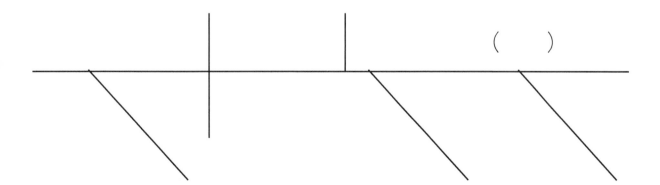

( )

You're never too old to learn.

Dictation

90

Narration

Narration

91

"I will go and get it. The room feels close."

She was too frightened.

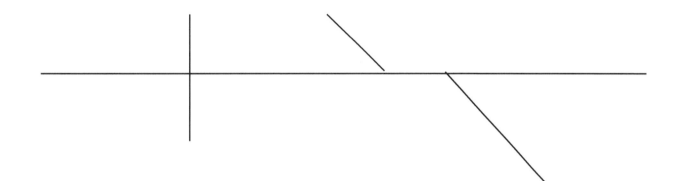

She looked up.

It was foolish indeed—thus to run farther and farther from all who could help her, as if she had been seeking a fit spot for the goblin-creature to eat her in at his leisure; but that is the way fear serves us: it always takes the side of the thing that we are afraid of.

Till a wind or water wrinkle,
  Dipping marten, plumping trout,
Spreads in a twinkle
And blots all out.

bank

broad

webbed

coarse

scramble

She remembered however that at night she spun only in the moonlight, and concluded that must be why there was no sweet, bee-like humming.

"Sit down again, Irene."

_____

"Oh! I do feel it!"

_____

In a few minutes the princess had sobbed herself to sleep. How long she slept, I do not know. When she came to herself she was sitting in her own high chair at the nursery table, with her doll's house before her.

When the cat's away the mice will play.

The father tore the fish with his teeth quite fiercely, and sometimes threw small pieces to the young ones, who had soon finished their tiny fish. At last all was eaten up, except the heads and tails.

She told her all about the cat with the long legs, and how she ran out upon the mountain, and came back again.

"Where have you been?"

"Oh, Lootie! I've had a

dreadful adventure!"

"Oh, Lootie! I've had such a dreadful adventure!" she replied, and told her all about the cat with the long legs, and how she ran out upon the mountain, and came back again. But she said nothing of her grandmother or her lamp.

Quitters never win and winners never quit.

94

He had been in a distant part

of his dominions all the winter.

"Why doesn't she want it now?"

The sentence becomes: She does not want it now why?

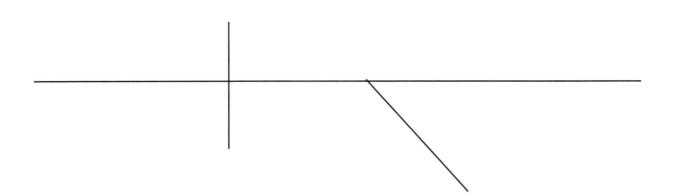

"I can't remember."

The king looked at it. A strange, beautiful smile spread like sunshine over his face, and an answering smile, but at the same time a questioning one, spread like moonlight over Irene's.

See the rings pursue each other;
All below grows black as night,
Just as if mother
Had blown out the light!

95

They had long bending bodies, and broad,
flat heads, and their mouths and noses
were short and broad. Their feet were
webbed like duck's feet, but each foot
had very sharp claws at the end. Their
fur was a lovely soft brown, but the long
hairs on the old otters were coarse, and
they did not look so soft as the little ones.
Their tails were thick and strong, and
very useful for helping them to swim.

"Pray what right have you in

my palace?"

She sat sideways.

Curdie ventured down.

Hope for the best, but prepare for the worst.

96

Narration

Narration

97

When she had passed through, the thread rose to about half her height, and she could hold it with ease as she walked.

She spied a dull red shine.

"When shall I wake?"

The sentence becomes: I shall wake when?

At length the thought struck her, that at least she could follow the thread backward, and thus get out of the mountain, and home. She rose at once, and found the thread. But the instant she tried to feel it backward, it vanished from her touch.

Patience, children, just a minute—
See the spreading circles die;
The stream and all in it
Will clear by-and-by.

peer

dart

minnow

perch

cradle

"Speak softly."

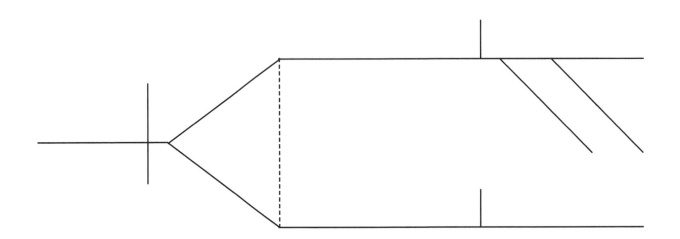

He had cleared a large

opening and followed her.

In a few moments he had cleared a large opening and followed her. They went on, down and down with the running water, Curdie getting more and more afraid it was leading them to some terrible gulf in the heart of the mountain.

When the going gets tough, the tough get going.

If all were rain and never sun,

No bow could span the hill;

If all were sun and never rain,

There'd be no rainbow still.

99

What would you see if I took you up

To my little nest in the air?

You would see the sky like a clear blue cup

Turned upside downwards there.

"I've brought Curdie, grandmother."

"He is a good boy, Curdie."

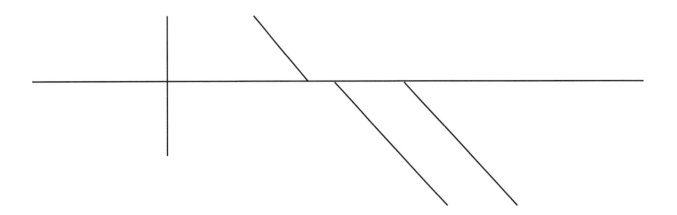

There was no answer when she knocked at length at the door of the workroom, nor could she hear any sound of the spinning-wheel, and once more her heart sank within her—but only for one moment, as she turned and knocked at the other door.

An ounce of prevention is worth a pound of cure.

100

"You must mind and keep out of the way of the men on the watch," said his mother.

"Oh, Curdie, they will see you."

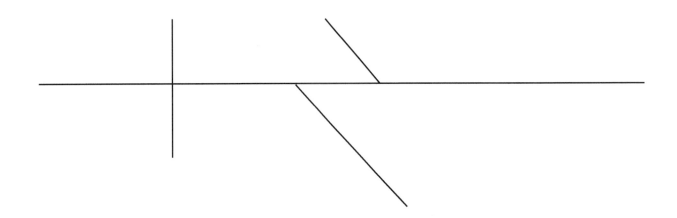

"I am sorry now."

Curdie went up the mountain neither whistling nor singing, for he was vexed with Irene for taking him in, as he called it; and he was vexed with himself for having spoken to her so angrily.

A diamond or a coal?
A diamond, if you please:
Who cares about a clumsy coal
Beneath the summer trees?

101

He has a bright blue streak down his back, his head and wings are a lovely green, with blue spots on the tips of the feathers. His beak is black. His chin and throat are white. He has a red streak behind his eye, with soft white feathers beyond, and his breast is shining like copper. Even his feet are red, and look quite gay against the dull branch.

From an island of the sea

Sounds a voice that summons me—

"Turn thy prow, sailor, come

With the wind home!"

"You are very rude, my dear

princess."

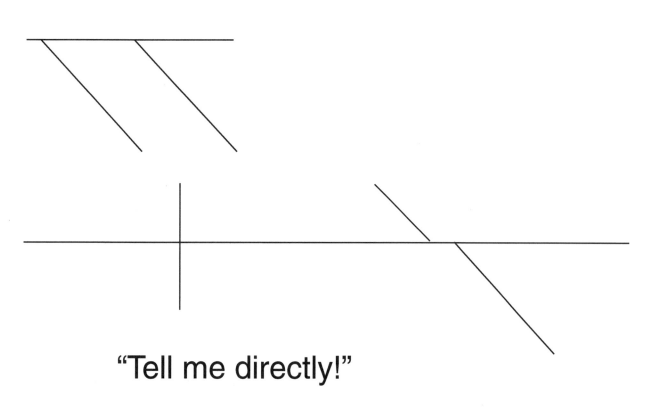

"Tell me directly!"

If you lie down with dogs, you'll get up with fleas.

102

Narration

103

The modest Rose puts forth a thorn,

The humble sheep a threat'ning horn:

While the Lily white shall in love delight,

Nor a thorn nor a threat stain her beauty bright.

The house quivered.

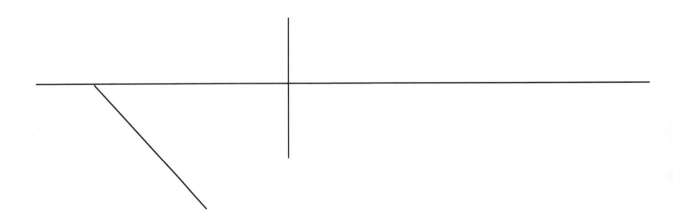

The housemaids had been listening.

"It seems to me," said the nurse, "that the noises are much too loud for that. I have heard them all day, and my princess has asked me several times what they could be."

A diamond or a coal?
A coal, sir, if you please:
One comes to care about the coal
What time the waters freeze.

nosegay

float

curious

root

rather

There is but one May in the year,

And sometimes May is wet and cold;

There is but one May in the year

Before the year grows old.

Yet though it be the chilliest May,

With least of sun and most of showers,

Its wind and dew, its night and day,

Bring up the flowers.

Away scattered the goblins in every direction—into closets, upstairs, into chimneys, up on rafters, and down to the cellars.

The queen gave a howl.

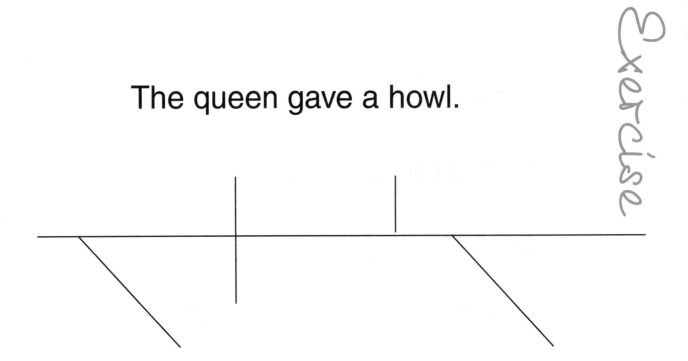

"Where's the princess?"

Can you remember what this sentence becomes?
Look at the bottom of the page if you need help!

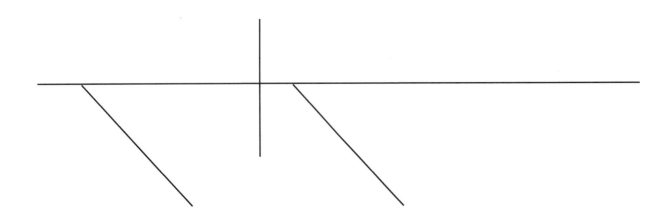

The princess is where?

He determined to find and rescue the princess as she had found and rescued him, or meet the worst fate to which the goblins could doom him.

People who live in glass houses shouldn't throw stones.

Maxim

One set her foot on the log. The other did likewise. In the middle they met horn to horn. Neither would give way, and so they both fell, to be swept away by the roaring torrent below. It is better to yield than to come to misfortune through stubbornness.

105

This hearth was built for thy delight,

For thee the logs were sawn,

For thee the largest chair, at night,

Is to the chimney drawn.

For thee, dear lass, the match was lit

To yield the ruddy blaze—

May Jack Frost give us joy of it

For many, many days.

The door was on the latch, and he entered. There sat his mother by the fire, and in her arms lay the princess fast asleep.

"Hush, Curdie!"

_____

_____

"Oh, Curdie! You're come!"

_____   _____

_____

"Poor Curdie! To lie there hurt and ill, and me never to know it!" exclaimed the princess, stroking his rough hand. "I would not have hesitated to come and nurse you, if they had told me."

The grass is always greener on the other side of the hill.

106

Rushes in a watery place,

And reeds in a hollow;

A soaring skylark in the sky,

A darting swallow;

And where pale blossom used to hang

Ripe fruit to follow.

The wind was blowing as

if it would blow him off the

mountain.

"I never had such fun!"

"They will be dreadfully frightened."

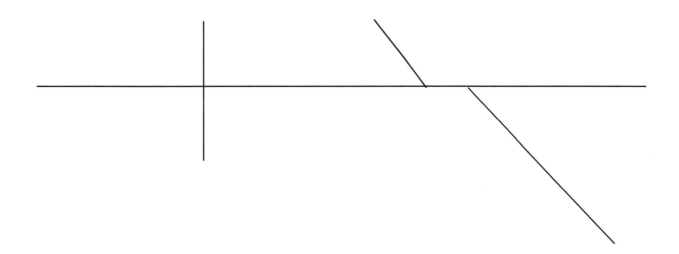

"It all depends on what kind your inside house is," said the mother.

"I know what you mean," said Irene. "That's the kind of thing my grandmother says."

Rushes in a watery place,
And reeds in a hollow;
A soaring skylark in the sky,
A darting swallow;
And where pale blossom used to hang
Ripe fruit to follow.

107

"See, Peter, I must have one of those lovely yellow 'water-lilies,' with its large, shiny green leaf, and one of its curious seed-boxes, which remain after the yellow flower-leaves have fallen off. I know that this plant has a thick stem in the mud at the bottom of the pond, and the long stalks grow right up, so that the leaves float on the top of the water. Little beetles crawl inside the flower and get honey from under the small yellow flower-leaves inside."

Strange that the city thoroughfare,

Noisy and bustling all the day,

Should with the night renounce its care

And lend itself to children's play!

Then they all went into the house, and the cook rushed to the kitchen, and the servants to their work.

"Oh, Curdie! My king-papa is come."

_____   _____

Curdie held up the princess.

Genius is one percent inspiration and ninety-nine percent perspiration.

108

Narration

_____
_____
_____
_____
_____
_____
_____
_____
_____
_____
_____
_____
_____
_____
_____
_____
_____
_____
_____
_____
_____
_____

Narration

Copywork

Made in United States
Troutdale, OR
08/27/2024

22329303R00250